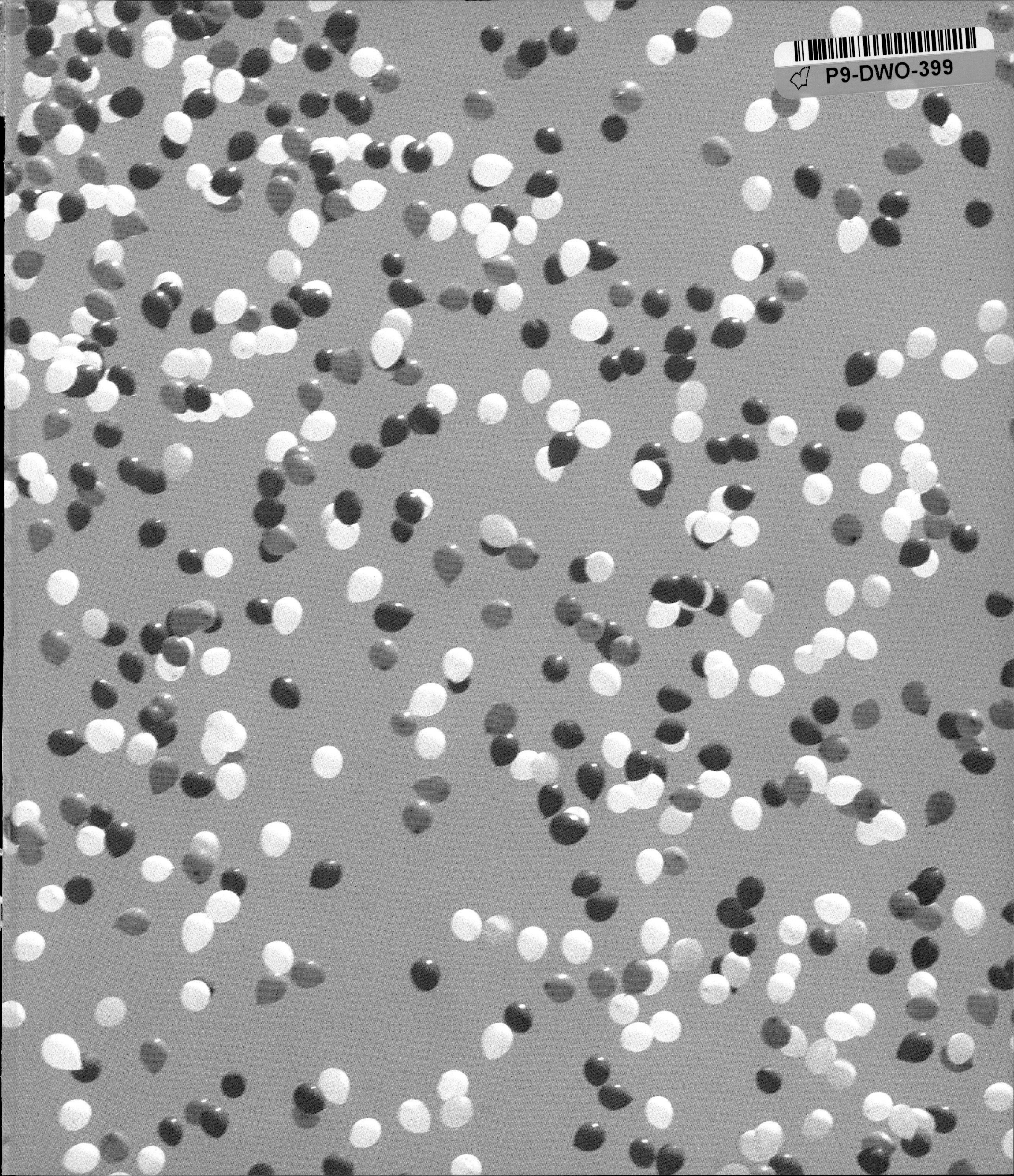

THIS IS MY HOME

A CELEBRATION OF CANADA

PAUL BELSERENE AND ROBIN LECKY

EDITORS

Creative House

Douglas & McIntyre
Vancouver/Toronto

Copyright © 1986 by Creative House (1985) Ltd.
86 87 88 89 90   5 4 3 2 1

Douglas & McIntyre Ltd.,
1615 Venables Street,
Vancouver, British Columbia V5L 2H1

Canadian Cataloguing in Publication Data
Main entry under title:
    This is my home
    ISBN 0-88894-517-5
    1. Canada – Description and travel – 1981 –
    – Views. 2. Canada Day – Pictorial works. *
    I. Creative House (Vancouver, B.C.)
    FC59.T58 1986   971.064'7'022   C86-091322-8
    F1017.T58 1986

Front jacket photograph by John Sleeman
Back jacket photograph by John Wyne
Design by Per Jacobsen and Design Projection
Studio Ltd.
Typeset by PolaGraphics Ltd.
Printed and bound in Canada by D. W. Friesen
& Sons Ltd.

THE FIRST OF JULY, Canada Day. At 5:03 A.M. a ray of sunlight touches a flag on Signal Hill, Newfoundland. From this beginning, the first of July moves west, at the speed of the sun, touching off pancake breakfasts, parades, ethnic dances, raft races, barbecues, cake cuttings, daytrips, beauty contests, concerts and family picnics across Canada. This is not a day like any other day. By the time twilight leaps across the Pacific from Vancouver Island, a finale of fireworks will have flown over nearly one billion hectares, illuminating twenty-five million upturned faces. This is Canada Day, and whoever we are, whatever we normally do, we are all a little bit different today. We are part of a Canadian celebration.

This Is My Home celebrates that celebration. What we have here is a pulling together of thousands of individual threads from every part of the country. The number of participants in the making of this book is enormous, and much of the spirit of *This Is My Home* comes from participants who would normally not think of themselves as contributors to a book: composers, musicians, set designers, computer programmers and audio engineers, in addition to writers, photographers and graphic artists. In fact what they, and we at Creative House, were setting out to create was a show – sound and motion, light and colour. Only later, to our delight, did we realize that we were also creating a book.

LE PREMIER JUILLET, Jour du Canada. À 5h03, un rayon de soleil touche un drapeau de Signal Hill, à Terre-Neuve. De là, on va vers l'ouest, à la vitesse du soleil, effleurant petits déjeuners et défilés, danses nationales et courses de radeaux, barbecues et excursions, concours de beauté et concerts, d'un bout à l'autre du Canada. C'est une journée exceptionnelle, et au moment où le crépuscule s'étend sur le Pacifique depuis l'île de Vancouver, une finale de feux d'artifice illumine vingt-cinq millions de visages. Qui que nous soyons, quelles que soient nos occupations habituelles, le Jour du Canada, nous devenons tous un peu différents.

On est chez nous célèbre cette journée et rassemble des centaines de participants de tous les coins du pays. En effet, l'esprit de *On est chez nous* provient de gens qui, générale-ment, ne collaborent pas à l'élaboration d'un livre – composi-teurs, musiciens, décorateurs de scène, programmeurs d'ordinateurs, ingénieurs du son, en plus, évidem-ment, des écrivains, photographes et concepteurs graphiques.

De fait, ce que toutes ces personnes et nous-mêmes, chez Creative House, nous étions engagés à faire, c'était un spectacle tout en sons et mouvements, lumières et couleurs. Plus tard seulement avons-nous compris, et quelle agréable surprise, que nous étions aussi en train de créer un livre.

Putting together the show *This Is My Home* for the Canada Pavilion at EXPO 86 was exciting, immensely satisfying and incredibly hard work. The original objective of the show was laid down by Norman Hay, Creative Director of the Canada Pavilion. The challenge was twofold. Create a stirring first impression of Canada for millions of international visitors coming to Vancouver, to EXPO 86 and to the Canada Pavilion. Awaken, at the same time, a spirit of pride among the Canadians who would come to feel that they were welcoming the world to their home.

We met this challenge in the five-hundred-seat semicircular Canada Celebration theatre, the introductory theatre for the Canada Pavilion. Our theatre was, in a very real sense, a rite of passage into Canada. The language of Norman Hay's call for proposals left no doubt as to the importance placed on the visitor's first experience of the pavilion. He said:

"During the six minutes of the Canada Celebration, visitors are to be treated to the most daring, dynamic and uplifting audiovisual performance about Canada and Canadians ever seen. The intent is to be unashamedly patriotic and emotional. It is necessary to find a new, fresh, creative way to present Canadians in a way that is moving, dramatic and joyous."

La production du spectacle *On est chez nous* pour le Pavillon du Canada à l'EXPO 86, a constitué un travail à la fois extrêmement ardu et satisfaisant. L'objectif original nous avait été expliqué par Norman Hay, directeur de la création du pavillon, et comportait un double défi. Il s'agissait de créer une première impression émouvante du Canada pour les millions de visiteurs internationaux venant à Vancouver, et de susciter aussi, chez les Canadiens, la fierté d'un peuple qui accueille le monde entier chez lui.

Nous avons relevé le défi dans le théâtre semi-circulaire de cinq-cents places "Célébration-Canada," qui est en somme le théâtre d'accueil du pavillon. D'ailleurs, les paroles de Norman Hay lors de son appel d'offres ne laissaient aucun doute sur l'importance qu'on devait donner à ce premier contact des visiteurs avec le pavillon. Il disait:

"Pendant les six minutes de 'Célébration-Canada,' les visiteurs doivent être transportés par le spectacle audio-visuel le plus audacieux, le plus dynamique et le plus enlevant jamais produit sur le Canada. Le but avoué est d'être franchement patriotique et émotif. Cela est nécessaire si on veut façonner une présentation nouvelle et inusitée des Canadiens, qui soit à la fois émouvante, dramatique et joyeuse."

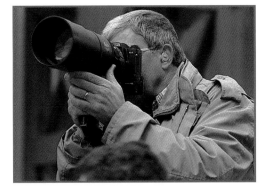

That was all. We could do anything we wanted, as long as it was daring, dynamic, uplifting, patriotic, emotional, moving, dramatic, joyous and, oh yes, in both official languages.

Poring over the blueprints for the theatre, we began to rough out the concept for the show, marrying our ideas to the architecture of the theatre. Gradually, the show's final format emerged: fourteen individual screens, three projectors per screen, forty-two projectors in all, interlocked with a quadraphonic sound system and special effects lighting.

Of course, as we worked, we let our imaginations fly. At one point we considered opening the show with the simulated aroma of morning coffee and closing it with a recreation of the Northern Lights. But we ultimately resolved that simplest was best.

And this particular concept was as simple as we could make it. We would let the people of Canada themselves show us what a celebration of Canada could be.

So that is how it came to pass that on the first of July, 1985, thirty-three photographers went out to villages, towns and cities, from sea to sea and from the southern border to the Arctic.

Et voilà, c'est tout. On pouvait faire ce qu'on voulait, à condition que ce soit audacieux, dynamique, patriotique, émouvant, émotif, dramatique, joyeux et, ah oui, que ce soit produit dans les deux langues officielles.

En étudiant les plans du théâtre, on a commencé à tracer les grandes lignes du spectacle, mariant nos idées à l'architecture de la salle. Graduellement, le format final se précisait: quatorze écrans individuels, trois projecteurs par écran soit un total de quarante-deux projecteurs, reliés à un système sonore quadraphonique et un éclairage à effets spéciaux.

Au cours de notre processus d'élaboration, nous avons laissé libre cours à notre imagination. À un certain moment, on a même pensé commencer le spectacle avec l'arôme du café, et le terminer avec une présentation d'aurores boréales. Mais nous avons finalement opté pour la simplicité.

Les Canadiens eux-mêmes nous montreraient ce que c'est qu'une célébration du Canada.

C'est ainsi que, le 1er juillet 1985, trente-trois photographes allaient dans les villes et villages du pays, croquer sur le vif les événements de la journée.

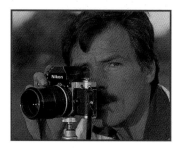

Some knew their areas well, others saw these parks, lakes and parade grounds for the first time through the lenses of their cameras. Manfred Buchheit went to Carbonear, and Don Robinson wandered between Margaree and Chéticamp. Alain Cornu, Paul Chiasson and John Sleeman fanned out from Montréal. John Bilodeau visited Canmore and Banff. David Barber lives in Ottawa but stayed with family while shooting Halifax. Ian Biggar needed directions to St. Paul. Linda Tamblyn, Creative House animation stand operator, picked up her 35-mm camera and went "on vacation" to Calgary, her old home. Gary Fiegehen of Vancouver was already on vacation at Sauble Beach, where he grew up. Kharen Hill, in Toronto for the first time in her life, but on a different assignment, took the first of July "off" for *This Is My Home*. Richard Hartmier decided to shoot around his home for as long as there was light, which in Whitehorse on the first of July means twenty-four hours.

Our instructions to our photographers were no less demanding than those of the Canada Pavilion to us:

"What we expect of you is easy to say, less easy to do. We want a large number of extraordinary photographs of all types of Canadians in all their activities and natural habitats on 1 July, 1985. We have

Certains connaissaient très bien leur région, d'autres voyaient parcs, lacs et parcours de défilés pour la première fois. Manfred Buchheit est allé à Carbonear, et Don Robinson s'est promené entre Margaree et Chéticamp. Alain Cornu, Paul Chiasson et John Sleeman sont partis de Montréal, couvrir la province. John Bilodeau a visité Canmore et Banff. David Barber habite Ottawa mais il a visité sa famille en prenant ses photos d'Halifax. Ian Biggar a dû se renseigner sur la façon de se rendre à St-Paul. Linda Tamblyn, la préposée au stand d'animation de Creative House, prenait son appareil 35-mm et partait "en vacances" à Calgary, son ancienne résidence. Gary Fiegehen de Vancouver était déjà en vacances à Sauble Beach, où il avait grandi. Kharen Hill, à Toronto pour la première fois de sa vie, décidait de "prendre congé" le premier juillet, pour *On est chez nous*. Richard Hartmier décidait de photographier les environs de chez lui tant qu'il y aurait de la lumière, ce qui veut dire pendant vingt-quatre heures, à Whitehorse, le premier juillet.

Nos directives aux photographes n'étaient pas moins exigeantes que celles du Pavillon du Canada envers nous:

"Ce que nous attendons de vous est facile à dire mais moins facile à réaliser. Nous voulons beaucoup de photos extraordinaires de tous les types de Canadiens et de leurs activités, le 1er juillet, dans leur région respective.

supplied you with a list of specific Canada Day events in your area and names of people you should contact. But we will expect you also to do your own backgrounding and research and to draw on your own contacts.

"Most of all, we expect you to reach into your own imagination. Because this is a multiscreen, multi-projector production, we have a voracious appetite for images and points of view. But please, no scenics. It is PEOPLE who will make this show. Your job is to catch these people in the act of celebrating Canada, however small or large that celebration may be."

We knew we were asking for a lot, but something in the tone of the many cross-country phone conversations we had as we readied thirty-three cameras and a thousand rolls of film in the last few days of June made us believe that we had struck a responsive chord in all of our photographers.

In the first week of July, as the film returned, we knew we had been right.

There were over thirty thousand images, thirty thousand tiny patches of colour. As we began sorting through this kaleidoscope of people and places, we began to piece together exactly what a Canada Celebration was.

"Nous vous avons fourni une liste d'événements particuliers du Jour du Canada dans votre région et les noms de personnes avec qui communiquer. Mais vous devrez faire votre propre recherche et prendre vos propres initiatives à partir de là.

"Mais surtout, nous voulons que vous fassiez appel à votre imagination. Parce que nous travaillons avec multi-écrans et multi-projecteurs, nous avons besoin d'un grand nombre d'images et d'une infinie variété de points de vue. S'il vous plaît, pas de paysages! Nous voulons du MONDE! Votre travail consiste à saisir les visages en pleine célébration, quelle qu'elle soit."

Nous savions que nous demandions beaucoup mais, au cours des nombreuses conversations téléphoniques transcontinentales des derniers jours de juin, au moment même où on préparait les mille rouleaux de film pour nos trente-trois photographes, quelque chose nous faisait croire que nous avions touché une corde sensible chez eux.

Et la première semaine de juillet, alors que les films commençaient à arriver, on savait qu'on avait eu raison.

Il y avait plus de trente mille images, trente mille petits carrés de couleur. Et en faisant notre choix parmi ce kaléidoscope de visages et de villes, on découvrait bientôt ce que c'était vraiment qu'une célébration du Canada.

Across the country, we saw, were common themes. There were pancake breakfasts in almost every town. Birthday cakes by the hundreds. Parades, politicians, popsicles and flags everywhere.

Of thirty thousand pictures, not a single one was posed. Not a single shot had been preplanned. Our photographers had accomplished the ultimate triumph of photojournalism: they had let their subjects be.

There were also differences, subtle differences, from region to region across the country: differences in the faces, in the crowds, in the essence of the moments our photographers captured. Somehow, though we had asked our photographers to concentrate on people rather than scenery, the scenery was there as well. And more. In the colour and the lighting, there was a touch of Christopher Pratt in the Maritimes, Ken Danby inhabited the busy-ness of Ontario and the pastel pink and purple sunsets of British Columbia were pure Toni Onley.

We knew we had tapped a vein of magic. And we knew that the magic would work in a book just as well as it would work in a theatre. The book *This Is My Home* is not the show *This Is My Home*. The show contains ten times the images in the book. To bring these images together we used a song, also entitled "This Is My Home," and a

D'un bout à l'autre du pays, on pouvait voir des thèmes communs. Dans presque toutes les villes, par exemple, on a trouvé des crêpes au petit déjeuner. On a vu des centaines de gâteaux d'anniversaire, et partout, politiciens, crème glacée et drapeaux faisaient partie du décor.

Trente mille images avaient été prises sur le vif. Personne n'avait "posé" pour aucune photo. Nos photographes avaient ainsi accompli un ultime triomphe de photojournalisme. Ils avaient laissé leurs sujets être eux-mêmes.

On a aussi remarqué des différences, de subtiles différences d'une région à l'autre. Dans les visages et dans les foules, dans l'essence même de certains moments. Et plus encore. Bien que l'on ait spécifié à nos photographes de concentrer leur attention sur les personnes et non pas sur les paysages, on a quand même trouvé des couleurs et des lumières qui nous rappelaient un Christopher Pratt dans les Maritimes, un Ken Danby dans l'activité de l'Ontario, et enfin, les couchés de soleil en rose et lilas de la Colombie-Britannique étaient du pur Toni Onley.

On savait qu'on avait touché une veine magique. Et on savait aussi que cette magie serait tout aussi évocatrice dans un livre que dans une salle de projection.

Le livre *On est chez nous* est différent du spectacle du même nom. Le spectacle contient en fait dix fois plus d'images que le livre et

symphonic soundtrack that leads the eye across all fourteen screens, across all ten provinces and two territories.

For the book, we went back to our photographers and asked them to recall the high points of that Canada Day shoot for us. Their words form the "soundtrack" that holds this book together. We also recognized that the people, places and colours of this book required, as well, the words and feelings of people who might find themselves on the other end of the camera. And so we asked Canadians, some well known, some not, to complete our story with their feelings, in their chosen language, about what it means to say "This is my home."

Canadians are not, by and large, a flagwaving people. We tend to be rather modest in our patriotism. Yet the feeling is there, and it runs deep. And the first of July is one day of the year, at least, when that feeling could fill a book, and more.

This is that book.

Paul Belserene
Robin Lecky

Editors

on y unifie les images par une chanson, elle aussi intitulée "On est chez nous," ainsi que par un arrangement symphonique. La bande sonore guide l'oeil d'un bout à l'autre des quatorze écrans, d'un océan à l'autre.

Pour le livre, nous sommes retournés à nos photographes et nous leur avons demandé de nous raconter les points saillants de la journée. Leurs mots sont la "bande sonore" qui unifie l'ouvrage. Nous avons aussi découvert que les visages, les endroits et les couleurs, qu'on retrouvait dans les images, avaient besoin d'être complétés par les mots et les sentiments d'autres personnes, certaines connues, d'autres pas, afin d'étoffer notre histoire par des paroles qui exprimaient leur fierté d'être canadiens.

Les Canadiens ne sont pas reconnus comme étant particulièrement patriotiques. De fait nous avons tendance à être plutôt modestes dans ce domaine. Cependant, le sentiment est là, et il est ancré en nous. Le premier juillet était une journée de l'année où ce sentiment pouvait remplir tout un livre, et même plus.

Voici ce livre.

Paul Belserene
Robin Lecky

Éditeurs

All of us involved in *This Is My Home* felt that these magical images of one day, one celebration, one people and one sentiment should endure beyond the six-month span of EXPO 86. It is impossible to list everyone who has made an unselfish contribution to *This Is My Home*, but it would be unforgivable to omit these few:

PAUL SMITH, Creative Director. Softspoken but determined, Paul was responsible for the original concept of *This Is My Home*, and for the guiding of this project through every phase of production. He brought all of its elements together into one spectacular multimedia experience, and he laid the foundation for translating that magic onto the printed page.

THE PHOTOGRAPHERS. Their names appear throughout the book, alongside their images, and, in many cases, beneath their quotations. It goes without saying that their work comprises the substance of this book. Just as importantly, however, their dedication, co-operation and understanding infuse its spirit.

Nous tous qui avons contribué à *On est chez nous* avons senti que ces images magiques d'un jour, d'une célébration, d'un peuple et d'un sentiment devraient pouvoir durer plus longtemps que les six mois d'EXPO 86. Il est impossible d'énumérer ici tous ceux qui ont généreusement contribué à *On est chez nous*, mais il serait impardonnable d'omettre les quelques personnes suivantes:

PAUL SMITH, Directeur de Création. Concepteur exceptionnel, il est responsable de l'idée originale de *On est chez nous* et il a guidé ce projet à travers toutes les phases de sa production. Il a rassemblé tous les éléments en une expérience multimedia spectaculaire, et a inspiré sa transposition imprimée.

LES PHOTOGRAPHES. Leurs noms apparaissent tout au long du livre, près des images qu'ils ont captées et, dans plusieurs cas aussi, sous leurs citations. Il va sans dire que leur oeuvre constitue l'essentiel de ce livre et que leur dévouement, leur coopération et leur compréhension ont enrichi l'esprit même de sa réalisation.

BRIAN GIBSON, Composer, Conductor. One day in August he haltingly sang us some lyrics that sent shivers down our spines. A few months later he was conducting over a hundred classical musicians, solo singers and the Vancouver Bach Children's Chorus. With ARIANE FRANCE SMITH collaborating on French lyrics, he put words and music to what might be another Canadian national anthem.

PER JACOBSEN, Graphic Designer. His unfailing taste and design sense grace both the show and this book.

NORMAN HAY, BERNARD LÉVEILLÉ AND DICK LOTT. These men from the Canada Pavilion displayed remarkable faith in our theatre project and gratifying support for this book.

BOB BUCKLEY, BARB DENNIS, MARY FRYMIRE, HARLEY MICHAILUCK, ROGER MONK, DANIELLE PAGÉ, DON RAMSAY, DIANE THOMAS AND TRUDY WOODCOCK. These people formed the nucleus of a production team that worked long days and long nights to bring *This Is My Home* to light.

Lastly, we all send our heartfelt thanks to those Canadians who shared their celebrations with us on the first of July.

BRIAN GIBSON, Compositeur et Chef d'orchestre. Un jour, en août 1985, il nous fredonnait des paroles qui nous ont ému. Quelques mois plus tard, il dirigeait plus d'une centaine de musiciens et chanteurs ainsi que la Vancouver Bach Children's Chorus. Avec ARIANE FRANCE SMITH, qui a conçu les paroles françaises, il a assemblé paroles et musique en ce qui pourrait être un nouvel hymne national.

PER JACOBSEN, Concepteur graphique. Son goût infaillible et son élégance graphique se retrouvent tant dans le spectacle que dans ce livre.

NORMAN HAY, BERNARD LÉVEILLÉ ET DICK LOTT, tous trois du Pavillon du Canada, ont démontré une confiance remarquable dans notre projet et un encouragement précieux dans la préparation du livre.

BOB BUCKLEY, BARB DENNIS, MARY FRYMIRE, HARLEY MICHAILUCK, ROGER MONK, DANIELLE PAGÉ, DON RAMSAY, DIANE THOMAS ET TRUDY WOODCOCK forment le noyau de l'équipe de production qui a travaillé de longues heures à la préparation du livre *On est chez nous*.

Et finalement, nous tenons à remercier tous les Canadiens qui ont partagé leurs célébrations avec nous en ce premier juillet.

I t started about 3:00 A.M. People were setting up chairs in pitch blackness. The wind was howling around the hill, and people were almost fighting their way up – Canada Day organizers, politicians, bikers. We were all going to watch the first rays of sun touch Canada on Canada Day. And I remember thinking, "This is the heritage of Canada; people coming together in a harsh environment." ⅃ Then, at 5:05 A.M., this pure event happens. The sun rises, the flag is raised on Signal Hill, and a group of people sing "O Canada." And the sun shines on these people.

David Sedman
Photographer

David Sedman

David Sedman

David Sedman

■ For many outsiders,
Canada appears to
be a kind of gullible
Gulliver of the North,
an irrelevant hunk
of geography on the
fringes of civilization.
But for those of us
lucky enough to be
Canadian, we know
that this is a country
blessed with the man-
date of heaven – a land
to build dreams on.■
Peter C. Newman
Author

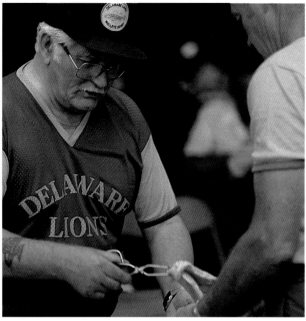

Claus Andersen

People had fun all day long. There was a nice feeling of togetherness, as well as enthusiasm about Canada Day. One man was mixing pancakes with a small, electric, one-horse-power outboard engine. He asked: "You're not from the food board, are you?"

Claus Andersen
Photographer

Ian Biggar

Paul Chiasson

■ I was thirteen years old when I became a Canadian. That was in 1949 when Newfoundland became the tenth province. It was like inheriting a four-million-square-mile backyard to play in; the promise of adventure, the feeling of security. And that's how it still is.■
Christopher Pratt
Artist

Gene Hattori

Claus Andersen

Claus Andersen

Ian Biggar

21

100 years
of heritage
conservation

1885

1985

■ J'ai vu mon pays comme aucun autre Canadien ne l'a vu. I have vaulted over an immense land which is both forbidding and beautiful and it took my breath away. There are no people more fortunate than we Canadians. We have received far more than our share.■
Marc Garneau
Astronaut

23

Just outside of Carbonear, Mr. Leonard Snow has created his magnificent yard art. Leonard has an incredible sense of patriotism and tradition. The red, white and blue that surround his house represent, to him, the old Newfoundland flag and the Union Jack.

Manfred Buchheit
Photographer

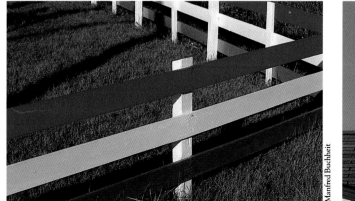

Wayne Barrett Anne Mackay

■ Canada is my home because: it works, however imperfectly and reluctantly; it has a social conscience which can be stirred to howl; it is utterly beautiful from sea to sea.■
June Callwood
Journalist

Wayne Barrett Anne Mackay

Peter Gross

David Barbour

Peter Gross

Don Robinson

■ Le Canada est une charnière entre l'ancienne Europe et le Nouveau Monde. C'est donc un pays de tous les possibles, où les cultures vieilles de mil ans peuvent prendre un nouveau souffle en terre d'avenir et de liberté.■
Antonine Maillet
Auteur

David Barbour

■ Canada means
freedom. The country
has given me a
freedom to develop,
freedom for those who
have listened to and
supported me and a
freedom to wave our
flag wherever I go,
something I do with
pride. ■
Corey Hart
Rock musician

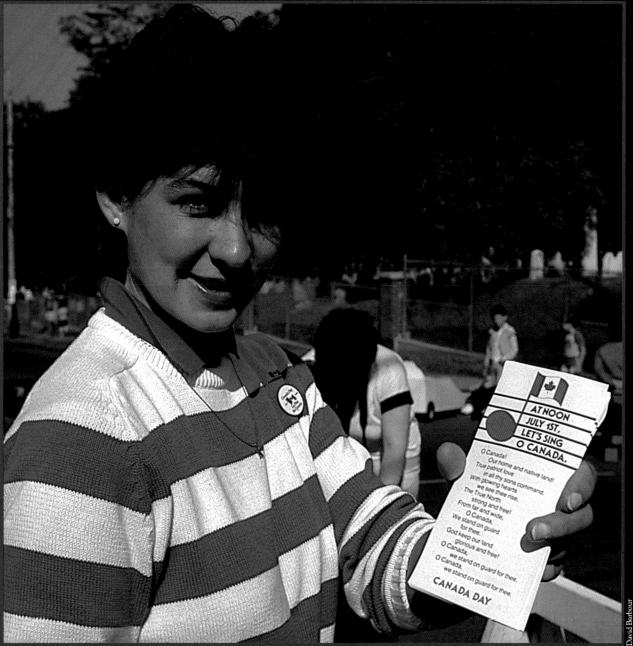

AT NOON
JULY 1ST,
LET'S SING
O CANADA.

O Canada!
Our home and native land!
True patriot love
in all thy sons command.
With glowing hearts
we see thee rise,
The True North,
strong and free!
From far and wide,
O Canada,
We stand on guard
for thee.
God keep our land
glorious and free!
O Canada,
we stand on guard for thee.
O Canada,
we stand on guard for thee.

CANADA DAY

David Barbour

Paul Chiasson

Paul Chiasson

Paul Chiasson

Paul Chiasson

Paul Chiasson

Paul Chiasson

■ Canada: a gigantic wonderland. The more I ramble through it and meet its incredibly diverse and interesting people, the more I believe all those high school clichés about the True North strong and free. ■
Michael Tenszen
Journalist

John Sleeman

Claus Andersen

Alain Cornu

Alain Cornu

■ Canada.
A chance to
be different and
enjoy it.■
*Phillippe Gaspé de
Beaubien
Media executive*

40

Je suis monté sur une table très instable. La Gendarmerie Royale me tenait pour m'empêcher de tomber sur le gâteau. Suivant le discours officiel, les enfants faisaient deux fois la queue pour du gâteau.

Alain Cornu
Photographe

■ Canada, as clumsy
as she sometimes is,
means well.■
Duncan MacPherson
Cartoonist

Ian Bigger

44

■ My home is my personal sanctuary, My retreat and haven, my castle. My home is my most comfortable territory, My studio and friends, my family. My home is Canada – my country. ■
Ken Danby
Artist

Ted Grant

Ted Grant

Ted Grant

■ Canada is the greatest country in the world . . .
and no one has ever argued this fact with me. ■
Angelo Mosca
Wrestling promoter

■ People see and hear my name and expect me to be from somewhere else. I'm proud to say I'm Canadian. No matter what country I compete in, the people cheer for Canadian skiers second only to their own.■
Liisa Savijarvi
Skier, Canadian
Olympic Team

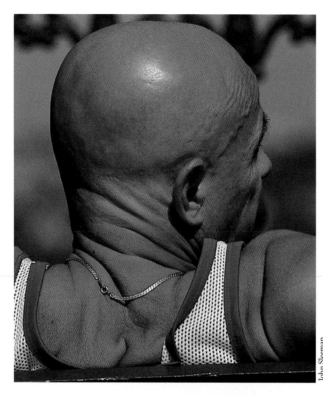

John Sleeman

John Sleeman

Paul Chiasson

John Sleeman

Paul Chiasson

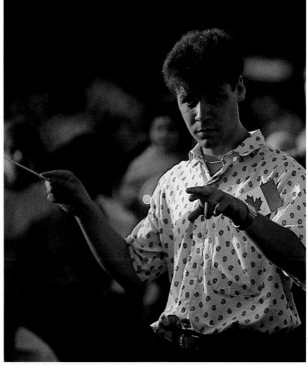

John Sleeman

■ La fierté canadienne pour moi, c'est d'avoir eu cette chance unique de faire honneur à mon pays lors des Jeux olympiques à Los Angeles. ■
*Sylvie Bernier
Plongeuse, Équipe canadienne olympique*

Paul Chiasson

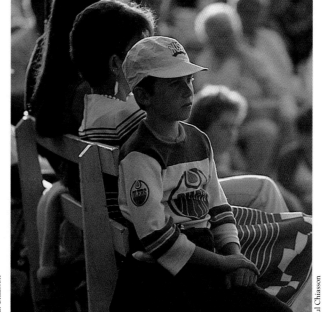

Paul Chiasson

49

George Gooderham

George Gooderham

I was in Elmira, Ontario, a small Mennonite community north of Kitchener. "Can I take your picture?"

George Gooderham

"I'm sorry but I can't pose for you as that would be vain." All Mennonites state this. "If you want to walk with me you can take pictures, but I can't pose for you."

George Gooderham

Photographer

Pierre St. Jacques

52

Pierre St. Jacques

■ I've served this great country during war and I have travelled extensively around the world, but the most peaceful experience I can think of is coming back home.■
S.H. Dunsdon
Dominion President
Royal Canadian Legion

Pierre St. Jacques

53

■ It's a pleasure to live in Canada, a country where no money is spent on weapons, where any woman can be a lawyer and where we queue for buses.■
Joyce Bradley
Lawyer

Kharen Hill

Kharen Hill

Kharen Hill

Bob Warren

Kharen Hill

Kharen Hill

Doug Fisher

■ Je connais son nom, son âge, ses saisons et ses paysages, mais je ne sais pas tout de son âme.■
Charlotte Duval
Auteur, compositeur, interprète

Pierre St. Jacques

■ The soul and vision of Canada lies in the ingenuity, imagination and courage of its people. In their faces I find the most profound mysteries and triumphs of the human spirit revealed, and a steady reassurance that in this imperfect world there exists a people who embrace and reflect in their daily lives the noble ideals of justice, compassion and freedom.■
Jeanne Sauvé
Governor General of
Canada

58

Pierre St. Jacques

Claus Andersen

Pierre St. Jacques

Pierre St. Jacques

■ Notre patrie, le Canada, est beaucoup plus qu'une entité géographique. Elle est, pourrait-on dire, un état d'âme et d'esprit, une façon de vivre qui conjugue l'ensemble des valeurs culturelles, sociales, linguistiques et religieuses et les exalte comme la richesse et la prospérité dont nous avons tous été si généreusement gratifiés. ■
Jeanne Sauvé
Le Gouverneur Général
du Canada

Gary Fiegehen

There is a home in everyone's heart, the place where they were a child. This project offered me the opportunity to revisit, participate and record Canada's birthday in the place of my childhood. It was an opportunity to see as a child again, to work from the heart and to work in bare feet.

Gary Fiegehen
Photographer

Ted Grant

Kharen Hill

■ All my intensities are defined by my roots, and my roots are entirely Canadian. I'm as Canadian as you'll ever find. ■
Donald Sutherland
Actor

Pierre St. Jacques

Barry Brooks

Anne Mackay

Wayne Barrett

Barry Brooks

Allan Harvey

George Gooderham

Allan Harvey

64

John Paskievich

I noticed the intensity of the celebration was inversely proportional to the time a person has been in Canada. I noticed the Vietnamese and Cambodians were more enthusiastic than the Ukrainians, who, in turn, were out in greater numbers than the native-born Canadians. Asians in particular were enjoying their new-found freedom to celebrate.

John Paskievich

Photographer

Brian Milne

■ Canada. Huge,
gentle and beautiful.■
Dr. Chin Charles Kwo
Acupuncturist

■ Canada is a country built on
dreams. Dreams of men and women
who came here from many of
the countries I have travelled
through. If you combine the
richness of the country with the
spirit of the people, our potential
as a nation is unlimited. ■
Rick Hansen
Athlete

Richard Gustin

John Bilodeau

Robert Brown   Linda Tamblyn

Robert Brown   Linda Tamblyn

John Bilodeau

■ I think Canada is populated with the funniest people in the world. I know I can't stop laughing.■
Vicki Gabereau
Broadcaster

John Bilodeau

John Paskievich

Pierre St. Jacques

Waiting for official ceremonies to begin in front of the legislature, it was a hot, hot day. One of the most interesting parts of the ceremony was watching and waiting to see if RCMP would faint in their wool suits. None did.

Richard Gustin
Photographer

Richard Gustin

Richard Gustin

Richard Gustin

Gene Hattori

■ Canada. Sometimes we have to wear two hats, but the greatest thing about Canada is that it's a place where we're allowed to express ourselves. ■
Chief Art Littlechild
Ermineskin Band

■ I feel fierce and strong being a Canadian.
We also have the cutest girls in the world. ■
Adiuto Pianosi
Businessman

John Bilodeau

Gerry Kopelow

Ian Biggar

John Bilodeau

John Bilodeau

John Bilodeau

78

■ Le Canada est une nation très diversifiée, mais où chacun se sent d'abord canadien. Pays multiple offrant maintes occasions et de nombreux défis, le Canada est nôtre et, comme notre foyer, nous sommes fiers de le partager. ■
Guy Chiasson
Vice président, Affaires publiques, Air Canada

John Wyne

Ian Biggar

The night before the shoot, my contacts in Mannville, Alberta, briefed me on what it was to be Canadian. With their help, I learned the words to "O Canada." ❧ So, Canada Day was the first day I sang "O Canada." It was after the ceremonies and the flag raising. ❧ The next day, I took the oath making me a Canadian citizen.

Ian Biggar

Photographer

Ian Biggar

Ian Biggar

Ian Biggar

Ian Biggar

■ Mon pays: c'est cette terre si riche.
Mon pays: ce sont ses gens pas exactement
comme les autres. Mon pays: c'est un passé
riche, un présent attirant, un avenir prometteur.
Mon pays: c'est vous, c'est moi, c'est le Canada. ■
Laurier LaPierre
Personnalité de la télévision

Andrew Klaver

■ I come from immigrant parents who
gave their lives to be a part of this great country.
They saw a future for their children here, a
vision that this would be the greatest country
in the world. ■
Jack Iwabuchi
Produce market executive

Robert Semeniuk

Doug Fisher

Allan Harvey

The annual Folk Fest parade was happening downtown. Various ethnic groups celebrated their adopted nationality as they marched towards Robson Square where a citizenship ceremony took place. This particular onlooker was more than tickled to gaze down the barrel of a wide-angle lens at close quarters, ensuring that his campaign ribbons filled the picture frame.

Allan Harvey
Photographer

Allan Harvey

■ A love affair that grows each passing year in fidelity, attachment, tenderness. One hungers for her when away. At home her loveliness is too much to caress, Canada lies open wide-eyed, expectant. Asking only for devotion, she wants to be possessed. ■
Justice John Matheson

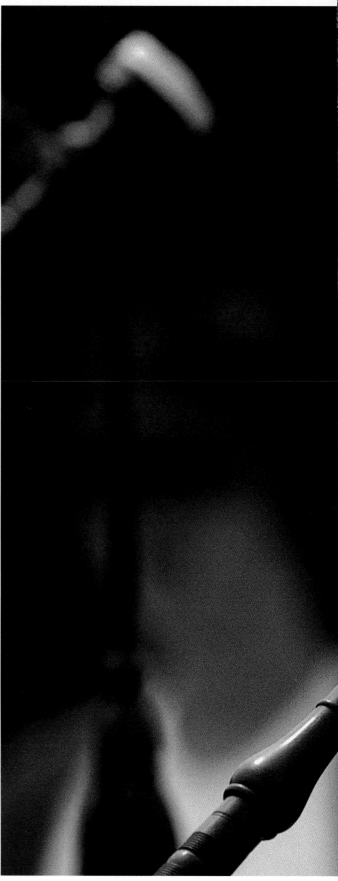

Ted Grant

Ted Grant

Ted Grant

The heat was stifling in Yellowknife. I'd dislocated my shoulder after fifteen hours and I couldn't sleep, so I shot twenty-four hours. It's so different here than in the south. There's a beautiful quality of light at 1:00 or 2:00 A.M. and kids are still playing in the streets.

Mike Beedell

Photographer

Mike Beedell

Mike Beedell

Mike Beedell

■ Canada's just the
absolute best. What
more can a guy living
in the Arctic say?■
Roger Davis
Mechanic

Mike Beedell

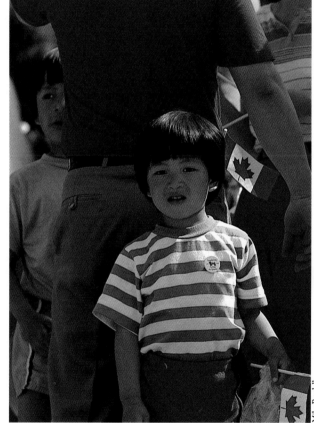

Mike Beedell

Mike Beedell

John Wyne

John Wyne

John Wyne

T he body building displays were held outdoors at Assiniboine Park, so you have to understand that everyone was getting bit by mosquitoes. They were drawn by the stage lighting. Women in the audience sat politely during the women's display, but when the men's display began, the women really let loose.

John Wyne

Photographer

Allan Harvey

John Wyne

Allan Harvey

Allan Harvey

94

Allan Harvey

Gerry Kopelow

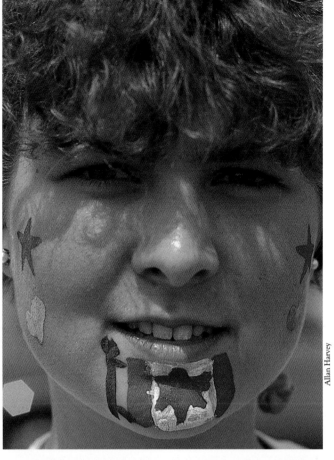

Allan Harvey

Andrew Klaver

■ Canada, what does it mean? I'm just so bloody proud of this country.■
Jim Dalzell
Reeve

■ Mon pays j'en suis
très orgueilleuse et, à
travers ma vie, je crois
avoir prouvé que je
suis avant tout
canadienne. ■
Jehane Benoît
Auteur, consultante en
alimentation

■ No matter how bad or negative things might appear, there's always a new horizon in Canada, something pulling this country of ours together. Canada is good therapy when you're feeling down. ■
Marc Cloutier
Real estate salesman

Bob Warren

For the people of Masset, the Canada Day celebration was a really big event. I was pretty excited because I had never been to a small town with such a delightful mix of people – native people, servicemen, fishermen, Sarah and Claude Davidson in their button blankets, and Little Miss Masset with her punk haircut with a streak of purple.

Andrew Klaver

Andrew Klaver

Andrew Klaver

■ I am always proud
of being a Canadian –
but I occasionally have
to leave and return to
truly appreciate how
great this country is.■
*Lucille Johnstone
President and Chief
Executive Officer
RivTow Straits Ltd.*

Andrew Klaver

■ My word on Canada comes from many years back from Gunnar Myrdal, the great Swedish economist and international statesman. It is thus free of parochial bias. He said that in his experience, Canada, considering its ethnic diversity and geographic breadth, was the best governed of the great nations of the world. My own thought: let it continue to be so, with, of course, a relentless will to improve.■
John Kenneth Galbraith
Economist

Andrew Klaver

Dawn Goss

■ Canadians enjoy the luxury of living in a land so large they can be friendly without being polite.■
Eric Nicol
Humourist

Brian Milne

I had two feelings about my Canada Day assignment. The first was a self-imposed competition with the other thirty-two photographers shooting for the same program. I wanted Victoria's celebration to look like the best celebration in the country and my photographs to blow everyone out of the water. ❡ The second most important feeling was my reaction when photographing the children. When I was a young boy, we had a holiday called Dominion Day. It didn't mean too much because we were already on a school summer holiday. Today it is called Canada Day. Now it means "my country and my home." The children I photographed in Victoria don't understand that yet, but they will.

Ted Grant

Photographer

Ted Grant

Ted Grant

■ Canada is a country that has not yet made up its mind on what it wants to be. I too do not know what I want to be. I like being Canadian because in this unfinished country I can make Canada dream along with me. Perhaps together we can make sure the best is yet to be.■

Larry Zolf
Broadcaster-journalist

Ted Grant

Pierre St. Jacques

Don Robinson

Wayne Barrett   Anne Mackay

Don Robinson

Lloyd Sutton

Kharen Hill

Ted Grant

Allan Harvey

■ I love this country because it is my home and my roots run deep. I share it with a tremendous variety of others from all over the globe. As we learn to work together to share our untold treasures of hand and mind and spirit, Canada can truly become a land of heart's desire. But that means learning to accept individual responsibility for change. Are we ready to learn?■
Grace MacInnis
Former Member of Parliament

Allan Harvey

MOLSON
GASTOWN GRAND P[...]
S T A R T / F I N I[...]

WINNING
MAGAZINE
7-ELEVEN
CUP SERIES
7-ELEVEN

MOLSO[...]

Barry Brooks

Barry Brooks

Barry Brooks

Barry Brooks

■ The thing I like most about this country is a sense of freedom I feel. (Get that in the book.) I've been to many other countries but coming home is a joy, something I look forward to. ■
Wayne Gretzky
Hockey player

We celebrate Canada Day a lot harder in the Yukon than anywhere else because the day is longer, and the summer is short, so we appreciate it a lot. We are tolerant of the southern bureaucrats who supply us with fireworks for Canada Day every year. They obviously don't know that we have a whole lot of light. Maybe they could send us larger noises and less of the coloured lights next year.

Richard Hartmier

Photographer

HAPPY 118th BIRTHDAY CANADA FROM YUKON DOG MUSHERS:
AL POPE, ANDY BUSBY, BEN LEFEBVRE, BILL HODGSON, DICK EASTMURE, SCOTT & DELORES SMITH, EDDIE LESCHART, ESA EKDAHL, JOHN BRYANT, KEN + JAN WEAGLE, PAUL SHERIDAN, BOB ENGLISH, JAN RUDOLPH, STEVE GIBBONS, SERGE SAWRENKO, STEVE GIBBONS, TARA SHERIDAN, MAUREEN DREW

Richard Hartmier

■ If you want to gauge how great Canada is, just go somewhere else and then think about what you left. I get a burr under my saddle when I hear people complaining about this land. ■
Cliff Paddington
Insurance agent

Richard Hartmier

Richard Hartmier

Richard Hartmier

John Bilodeau

David Barbour

David Barbour

Allan Harvey

Claus Andersen

■ I've always favoured black light, as opposed to the white, glittering light of California. I love painting clouds, and here in Canada you have all the clouds you could want. Anyway, if you don't like the weather, it will change in fifteen minutes.■
Toni Onley
Artist

Albert Normandin

■ In Canada, hardships are few and rewards great. You can attain what you strive for within its safe borders. ■
Ella Mang
Farmer

John Sleeman

■ Quand il faudra chercher le dernier îlot de liberté et de paix, c'est au Canada qu'on le trouvera.■
Hélène-Andrée Bizier
Historienne

John Sleeman

Lloyd Sutton

■ I've had many wonderful opportunities as a Canadian, both as an artist and a citizen. We live in paradise.■
Maureen Forrester
Chairman, Canada
Council

Pierre St. Jacques

Lloyd Sutton

Kharen Hill

■ Canada . . . I guess
you can't find too
many faults with it,
eh? That about sums
it up, eh?■
David Eagan
Fisherman

Kharen Hill

Barry Brooks

I t's not the red and white blowing in the wind that's really important. What's really important is the hands and the faces of the men holding the flags. ❡ So, as a photographer, part of the problem you face with a project like this is getting at something more elemental, less rehearsed. Chances are you'll find it before the parade starts, or off in the wings. It's the sharing of a vision not quite conceived – the attempt to act out a vision that no one is really sure of.

Barry Brooks

Photographer

David Sedman